In order to have a successful day-after-day Self Anxiety Therapy SAT you have to start with one thing: you must be in good terms with all the people which are the most important for you emotionally. They are not so numerous. 1? 2? 3? So start with reconciliation, when necessary. And then continue day after day during 7 to 14 days (7 days should be enough for anxiety disorder shorter than 1 year).

Week One

Day 1

Morning

* Repeat STOP (10 times every 30 min)

* Say slowly every hour: sun, flower, seven, path, tee, run, yellow, apple, fish, rain, pen, water, smile, talk, life, sky.

* Small physical excercise (10 min)

* Small breakfast.

* Nice talk (no complaints) 20 min. When nobody to talk with, phone or internet conversation oral or written.

* Walk 15 min.

* Imagine all the time people cannot wait to love you, but you must make the first step- a smile, a nice word or both. Only this! Do not be ashamed!

***

Afternoon

* Repeat STOP (10 times every 30 min.)

* Say slowly every hour: sun, flower, seven, path, tee, run, yellow, apple, fish, rain, pen, water, smile, talk, life, sky.

* Dinner and half an hour break (you can sleep).

* Nice talk (no complaints) 30 min. When nobody to talk with, phone or internet conversation oral or written.

* Walk 15 min.

* Imagine all the time people cannot wait to love you, but you must make the first step- a smile, a nice word or both. Only this! Do not be ashamed!

***

Evening

• Repeat STOP (10 times every 30 min.)

- Say slowly every hour: sun, flower, seven, path, tee, run, yellow, apple, fish, rain, pen, water, smile, talk, life, sky.
- Small supper.
- Nice talk (no complaints) 20 min. When nobody to talk with, phone or internet conversation oral or written.
- Walk 15 min.
- Imagine all the time people cannot wait to love you, but you must make the first step- a smile, a nice word or both. Only this! Do not be ashamed!

***

Night

Before sleep

- Take a shower (warm water) 1 min.
- Small physical excercise 3 min.

In Bed

- Repeat STOP (20 times)
- Say slowly untill you fall asleep: sun, flower, seven, path, tee, run, yellow, apple, fish, rain, pen, water, smile, talk, life, sky.

If you cannot fall asleep

- Say slowly untill you fall asleep: sun, flower, seven, path, tee, run, yellow, apple, fish, rain, pen, water, smile, talk, life, sky.

If above does not help

- Stand up and go to the toilet (when possible with as little light as possible)
- Say slowly untill you fall asleep: sun, flower, seven, path, tee, run, yellow, apple, fish, rain, pen, water, smile, talk, life, sky.

If above does not help

- Say STOP untill you fall asleep

If above does not help

- Go to the kitchen and have a very small snack.
- Back to the bed say slowly untill you fall asleep: sun, flower, seven, path, tee, run, yellow, apple, fish, rain, pen, water, smile, talk, life, sky.

If above does not help

- Say slowly untill morning: sun, flower, seven, path, tee, run, yellow, apple, fish, rain, pen, water, smile, talk, life, sky.

***

Day 2

Morning

* Repeat STOP (10 times every 30 min)

* Say slowly every hour: sun, flower, seven, path, tee, run, yellow, apple, fish, rain, pen, water, smile, talk, life, sky.

* Small physical excercise (10 min)

* Small breakfast.

* Nice talk (no complaints) 20 min. When nobody to talk with, phone or internet conversation oral or written.

* Walk 15 min.

* Imagine all the time people cannot wait to love you, but you must make the first step- a smile, a nice word or both. Only this! Do not be ashamed!

***

Afternoon

* Repeat STOP (10 times every 30 min.)

* Say slowly every hour: sun, flower, seven, path, tee, run, yellow, apple, fish, rain, pen, water, smile, talk, life, sky.

* Dinner and half an hour break (you can sleep).

* Nice talk (no complaints) 30 min. When nobody to talk with, phone or internet conversation oral or written.

* Walk 15 min.

* Imagine all the time people cannot wait to love you, but you must make the first step- a smile, a nice word or both. Only this! Do not be ashamed!

***

Evening

- Repeat STOP (10 times every 30 min.)
- Say slowly every hour: sun, flower, seven, path, tee, run, yellow, apple, fish, rain, pen, water, smile, talk, life, sky.
- Small supper.
- Nice talk (no complaints) 20 min. When nobody to talk with, phone or internet conversation oral or written.
- Walk 15 min.
- Imagine all the time people cannot wait to love you, but you must make the first step- a smile, a nice word or both. Only this! Do not be ashamed!

***

Night

Before sleep

- Take a shower (warm water) 1 min.
- Small physical excercise 3 min.

In Bed

- Repeat STOP (20 times)
- Say slowly untill you fall asleep: sun, flower, seven, path, tee, run, yellow, apple, fish, rain, pen, water, smile, talk, life, sky.

If you cannot fall asleep

- Say slowly untill you fall asleep: sun, flower, seven, path, tee, run, yellow, apple, fish, rain, pen, water, smile, talk, life, sky.

If above does not help

- Stand up and go to the toilet (when possible with as little light as possible)
- Say slowly untill you fall asleep: sun, flower, seven, path, tee, run, yellow, apple, fish, rain, pen, water, smile, talk, life, sky.

If above does not help

- Say STOP untill you fall asleep

If above does not help

- Go to the kitchen and have a very small snack.
- Back to the bed say slowly untill you fall asleep: sun, flower, seven, path, tee, run, yellow, apple, fish, rain, pen, water, smile, talk, life, sky.

If above does not help

- Say slowly untill morning: sun, flower, seven, path, tee, run, yellow, apple, fish, rain, pen, water, smile, talk, life, sky.

***

Day 3

Morning

* Repeat STOP (10 times every 30 min)

* Say slowly every hour: sun, flower, seven, path, tee, run, yellow, apple, fish, rain, pen, water, smile, talk, life, sky.

* Small physical excercise (10 min)

* Small breakfast.

* Nice talk (no complaints) 20 min. When nobody to talk with, phone or internet conversation oral or written.

* Walk 15 min.

* Imagine all the time people cannot wait to love you, but you must make the first step- a smile, a nice word or both. Only this! Do not be ashamed!

***

Afternoon

* Repeat STOP (10 times every 30 min.)

* Say slowly every hour: sun, flower, seven, path, tee, run, yellow, apple, fish, rain, pen, water, smile, talk, life, sky.

* Dinner and half an hour break (you can sleep).

* Nice talk (no complaints) 30 min. When nobody to talk with, phone or internet conversation oral or written.

* Walk 15 min.

* Imagine all the time people cannot wait to love you, but you must make the first step- a smile, a nice word or both. Only this! Do not be ashamed!

***

Evening

  • Repeat STOP (10 times every 30 min.)

- Say slowly every hour: sun, flower, seven, path, tee, run, yellow, apple, fish, rain, pen, water, smile, talk, life, sky.
- Small supper.
- Nice talk (no complaints) 20 min. When nobody to talk with, phone or internet conversation oral or written.
- Walk 15 min.
- Imagine all the time people cannot wait to love you, but you must make the first step- a smile, a nice word or both. Only this! Do not be ashamed!

***

Night

Before sleep

- Take a shower (warm water) 1 min.
- Small physical excercise 3 min.

In Bed

- Repeat STOP (20 times)
- Say slowly untill you fall asleep: sun, flower, seven, path, tee, run, yellow, apple, fish, rain, pen, water, smile, talk, life, sky.

If you cannot fall asleep

- Say slowly untill you fall asleep: sun, flower, seven, path, tee, run, yellow, apple, fish, rain, pen, water, smile, talk, life, sky.

If above does not help

- Stand up and go to the toilet (when possible with as little light as possible)
- Say slowly untill you fall asleep: sun, flower, seven, path, tee, run, yellow, apple, fish, rain, pen, water, smile, talk, life, sky.

If above does not help

- Say STOP untill you fall asleep

If above does not help

- Go to the kitchen and have a very small snack.
- Back to the bed say slowly untill you fall asleep: sun, flower, seven, path, tee, run, yellow, apple, fish, rain, pen, water, smile, talk, life, sky.

If above does not help

- Say slowly untill morning: sun, flower, seven, path, tee, run, yellow, apple, fish, rain, pen, water, smile, talk, life, sky.

***

Day 4

Morning

* Repeat STOP (10 times every 30 min)

* Say slowly every hour: sun, flower, seven, path, tee, run, yellow, apple, fish, rain, pen, water, smile, talk, life, sky.

* Small physical excercise (10 min)

* Small breakfast.

* Nice talk (no complaints) 20 min. When nobody to talk with, phone or internet conversation oral or written.

* Walk 15 min.

* Imagine all the time people cannot wait to love you, but you must make the first step- a smile, a nice word or both. Only this! Do not be ashamed!

***

Afternoon

* Repeat STOP (10 times every 30 min.)

* Say slowly every hour: sun, flower, seven, path, tee, run, yellow, apple, fish, rain, pen, water, smile, talk, life, sky.

* Dinner and half an hour break (you can sleep).

* Nice talk (no complaints) 30 min. When nobody to talk with, phone or internet conversation oral or written.

* Walk 15 min.

* Imagine all the time people cannot wait to love you, but you must make the first step- a smile, a nice word or both. Only this! Do not be ashamed!

***

Evening

- Repeat STOP (10 times every 30 min.)
- Say slowly every hour: sun, flower, seven, path, tee, run, yellow, apple, fish, rain, pen, water, smile, talk, life, sky.
- Small supper.
- Nice talk (no complaints) 20 min. When nobody to talk with, phone or internet conversation oral or written.
- Walk 15 min.
- Imagine all the time people cannot wait to love you, but you must make the first step- a smile, a nice word or both. Only this! Do not be ashamed!

***

Night

Before sleep

- Take a shower (warm water) 1 min.
- Small physical excercise 3 min.

In Bed

- Repeat STOP (20 times)
- Say slowly untill you fall asleep: sun, flower, seven, path, tee, run, yellow, apple, fish, rain, pen, water, smile, talk, life, sky.

If you cannot fall asleep

- Say slowly untill you fall asleep: sun, flower, seven, path, tee, run, yellow, apple, fish, rain, pen, water, smile, talk, life, sky.

If above does not help

- Stand up and go to the toilet (when possible with as little light as possible)
- Say slowly untill you fall asleep: sun, flower, seven, path, tee, run, yellow, apple, fish, rain, pen, water, smile, talk, life, sky.

If above does not help

- Say STOP untill you fall asleep

If above does not help

- Go to the kitchen and have a very small snack.
- Back to the bed say slowly untill you fall asleep: sun, flower, seven, path, tee, run, yellow, apple, fish, rain, pen, water, smile, talk, life, sky.

If above does not help

- Say slowly untill morning: sun, flower, seven, path, tee, run, yellow, apple, fish, rain, pen, water, smile, talk, life, sky.

***

Day 5

Morning

* Repeat STOP (10 times every 30 min)

* Say slowly every hour: sun, flower, seven, path, tee, run, yellow, apple, fish, rain, pen, water, smile, talk, life, sky.

* Small physical excercise (10 min)

* Small breakfast.

* Nice talk (no complaints) 20 min. When nobody to talk with, phone or internet conversation oral or written.

* Walk 15 min.

* Imagine all the time people cannot wait to love you, but you must make the first step- a smile, a nice word or both. Only this! Do not be ashamed!

***

Afternoon

* Repeat STOP (10 times every 30 min.)

* Say slowly every hour: sun, flower, seven, path, tee, run, yellow, apple, fish, rain, pen, water, smile, talk, life, sky.

* Dinner and half an hour break (you can sleep).

* Nice talk (no complaints) 30 min. When nobody to talk with, phone or internet conversation oral or written.

* Walk 15 min.

* Imagine all the time people cannot wait to love you, but you must make the first step- a smile, a nice word or both. Only this! Do not be ashamed!

***

Evening

• Repeat STOP (10 times every 30 min.)

- Say slowly every hour: sun, flower, seven, path, tee, run, yellow, apple, fish, rain, pen, water, smile, talk, life, sky.
- Small supper.
- Nice talk (no complaints) 20 min. When nobody to talk with, phone or internet conversation oral or written.
- Walk 15 min.
- Imagine all the time people cannot wait to love you, but you must make the first step- a smile, a nice word or both. Only this! Do not be ashamed!

***

Night

Before sleep

- Take a shower (warm water) 1 min.
- Small physical excercise 3 min.

In Bed

- Repeat STOP (20 times)
- Say slowly untill you fall asleep: sun, flower, seven, path, tee, run, yellow, apple, fish, rain, pen, water, smile, talk, life, sky.

If you cannot fall asleep

- Say slowly untill you fall asleep: sun, flower, seven, path, tee, run, yellow, apple, fish, rain, pen, water, smile, talk, life, sky.

If above does not help

- Stand up and go to the toilet (when possible with as little light as possible)
- Say slowly untill you fall asleep: sun, flower, seven, path, tee, run, yellow, apple, fish, rain, pen, water, smile, talk, life, sky.

If above does not help

- Say STOP untill you fall asleep

If above does not help

- Go to the kitchen and have a very small snack.
- Back to the bed say slowly untill you fall asleep: sun, flower, seven, path, tee, run, yellow, apple, fish, rain, pen, water, smile, talk, life, sky.

If above does not help

- Say slowly untill morning: sun, flower, seven, path, tee, run, yellow, apple, fish, rain, pen, water, smile, talk, life, sky.

***

Day 6

Morning

* Repeat STOP (10 times every 30 min)

* Say slowly every hour: sun, flower, seven, path, tee, run, yellow, apple, fish, rain, pen, water, smile, talk, life, sky.

* Small physical excercise (10 min)

* Small breakfast.

* Nice talk (no complaints) 20 min. When nobody to talk with, phone or internet conversation oral or written.

* Walk 15 min.

* Imagine all the time people cannot wait to love you, but you must make the first step- a smile, a nice word or both. Only this! Do not be ashamed!

***

Afternoon

* Repeat STOP (10 times every 30 min.)

* Say slowly every hour: sun, flower, seven, path, tee, run, yellow, apple, fish, rain, pen, water, smile, talk, life, sky.

* Dinner and half an hour break (you can sleep).

* Nice talk (no complaints) 30 min. When nobody to talk with, phone or internet conversation oral or written.

* Walk 15 min.

* Imagine all the time people cannot wait to love you, but you must make the first step- a smile, a nice word or both. Only this! Do not be ashamed!

***

Evening

- Repeat STOP (10 times every 30 min.)
- Say slowly every hour: sun, flower, seven, path, tee, run, yellow, apple, fish, rain, pen, water, smile, talk, life, sky.
- Small supper.
- Nice talk (no complaints) 20 min. When nobody to talk with, phone or internet conversation oral or written.
- Walk 15 min.
- Imagine all the time people cannot wait to love you, but you must make the first step- a smile, a nice word or both. Only this! Do not be ashamed!

***

Night

Before sleep

- Take a shower (warm water) 1 min.
- Small physical excercise 3 min.

In Bed

- Repeat STOP (20 times)
- Say slowly untill you fall asleep: sun, flower, seven, path, tee, run, yellow, apple, fish, rain, pen, water, smile, talk, life, sky.

If you cannot fall asleep

- Say slowly untill you fall asleep: sun, flower, seven, path, tee, run, yellow, apple, fish, rain, pen, water, smile, talk, life, sky.

If above does not help

- Stand up and go to the toilet (when possible with as little light as possible)
- Say slowly untill you fall asleep: sun, flower, seven, path, tee, run, yellow, apple, fish, rain, pen, water, smile, talk, life, sky.

If above does not help

- Say STOP untill you fall asleep

If above does not help

- Go to the kitchen and have a very small snack.
- Back to the bed say slowly untill you fall asleep: sun, flower, seven, path, tee, run, yellow, apple, fish, rain, pen, water, smile, talk, life, sky.

If above does not help

- Say slowly untill morning: sun, flower, seven, path, tee, run, yellow, apple, fish, rain, pen, water, smile, talk, life, sky.

***

Day 7

Morning

* Repeat STOP (10 times every 30 min)

* Say slowly every hour: sun, flower, seven, path, tee, run, yellow, apple, fish, rain, pen, water, smile, talk, life, sky.

* Small physical excercise (10 min)

* Small breakfast.

* Nice talk (no complaints) 20 min. When nobody to talk with, phone or internet conversation oral or written.

* Walk 15 min.

* Imagine all the time people cannot wait to love you, but you must make the first step- a smile, a nice word or both. Only this! Do not be ashamed!

***

Afternoon

* Repeat STOP (10 times every 30 min.)

* Say slowly every hour: sun, flower, seven, path, tee, run, yellow, apple, fish, rain, pen, water, smile, talk, life, sky.

* Dinner and half an hour break (you can sleep).

* Nice talk (no complaints) 30 min. When nobody to talk with, phone or internet conversation oral or written.

* Walk 15 min.

* Imagine all the time people cannot wait to love you, but you must make the first step- a smile, a nice word or both. Only this! Do not be ashamed!

***

Evening

* Repeat STOP (10 times every 30 min.)

- Say slowly every hour: sun, flower, seven, path, tee, run, yellow, apple, fish, rain, pen, water, smile, talk, life, sky.
- Small supper.
- Nice talk (no complaints) 20 min. When nobody to talk with, phone or internet conversation oral or written.
- Walk 15 min.
- Imagine all the time people cannot wait to love you, but you must make the first step- a smile, a nice word or both. Only this! Do not be ashamed!

***

Night

Before sleep

- Take a shower (warm water) 1 min.
- Small physical excercise 3 min.

In Bed

- Repeat STOP (20 times)
- Say slowly untill you fall asleep: sun, flower, seven, path, tee, run, yellow, apple, fish, rain, pen, water, smile, talk, life, sky.

If you cannot fall asleep

- Say slowly untill you fall asleep: sun, flower, seven, path, tee, run, yellow, apple, fish, rain, pen, water, smile, talk, life, sky.

If above does not help

- Stand up and go to the toilet (when possible with as little light as possible)
- Say slowly untill you fall asleep: sun, flower, seven, path, tee, run, yellow, apple, fish, rain, pen, water, smile, talk, life, sky.

If above does not help

- Say STOP untill you fall asleep

If above does not help

- Go to the kitchen and have a very small snack.
- Back to the bed say slowly untill you fall asleep: sun, flower, seven, path, tee, run, yellow, apple, fish, rain, pen, water, smile, talk, life, sky.

If above does not help

- Say slowly untill morning: sun, flower, seven, path, tee, run, yellow, apple, fish, rain, pen, water, smile, talk, life, sky.

***

Week Two

***

Day 1

Morning

* Repeat STOP (10 times every hour)

* Say slowly every 2 hours: sun, flower, seven, path, tee, run, yellow, apple, fish, rain, pen, water, smile, talk, life, sky.

* Small physical excercise (20 min)

* Small breakfast.

* Nice talk (no complaints) 30 min. When nobody to talk with, phone or internet conversation oral or written.

* Walk 30 min.

* Imagine all the time people cannot wait to love you, but you must make the first step- a smile, a nice word or both. Only this! Do not be ashamed!

***

Afternoon

* Repeat STOP (10 times every hour)

* Say slowly every 2 hours: sun, flower, seven, path, tee, run, yellow, apple, fish, rain, pen, water, smile, talk, life, sky.

* Dinner and half an hour break (you can sleep).

* Nice talk (no complaints) 30 min. When nobody to talk with, phone or internet conversation oral or written.

* Walk 30 min.

* Imagine all the time people cannot wait to love you, but you must make the first step- a smile, a nice word or both. Only this! Do not be ashamed!

***

Evening

- Repeat STOP to stop thinking.
- Say slowly to stop thinking: sun, flower, seven, path, tee, run, yellow, apple, fish, rain, pen, water, smile, talk, life, sky.
- Small supper.
- Nice talk (no complaints) 30 min. When nobody to talk with, phone or internet conversation oral or written.
- Walk 20 min.
- Imagine all the time people cannot wait to love you, but you must make the first step- a smile, a nice word or both. Only this! Do not be ashamed!

***

Night

Before sleep

- Take a shower (warm water) 1 min.
- Small physical excercise 5 min.

In Bed

- Repeat STOP (20 times)
- Say slowly untill you fall asleep: sun, flower, seven, path, tee, run, yellow, apple, fish, rain, pen, water, smile, talk, life, sky.

If you cannot fall asleep

- Say slowly untill you fall asleep: sun, flower, seven, path, tee, run, yellow, apple, fish, rain, pen, water, smile, talk, life, sky.

If above does not help

- Stand up and go to the toilet (when possible with as little light as possible)
- Say slowly untill you fall asleep: sun, flower, seven, path, tee, run, yellow, apple, fish, rain, pen, water, smile, talk, life, sky.

If above does not help

- Say STOP untill you fall asleep

If above does not help

- Go to the kitchen and have a very small snack.
- Back to the bed say slowly untill you fall asleep: sun, flower, seven, path, tee, run, yellow, apple, fish, rain, pen, water, smile, talk, life, sky.

If above does not help

- Say slowly untill morning: sun, flower, seven, path, tee, run, yellow, apple, fish, rain, pen, water, smile, talk, life, sky.

***

Day 2

Morning

* Repeat STOP (10 times every hour)

* Say slowly every 2 hours: sun, flower, seven, path, tee, run, yellow, apple, fish, rain, pen, water, smile, talk, life, sky.

* Small physical excercise (20 min)

* Small breakfast.

* Nice talk (no complaints) 30 min. When nobody to talk with, phone or internet conversation oral or written.

* Walk 30 min.

* Imagine all the time people cannot wait to love you, but you must make the first step- a smile, a nice word or both. Only this! Do not be ashamed!

***

Afternoon

* Repeat STOP (10 times every hour)

* Say slowly every 2 hours: sun, flower, seven, path, tee, run, yellow, apple, fish, rain, pen, water, smile, talk, life, sky.

* Dinner and half an hour break (you can sleep).

* Nice talk (no complaints) 30 min. When nobody to talk with, phone or internet conversation oral or written.

* Walk 30 min.

* Imagine all the time people cannot wait to love you, but you must make the first step- a smile, a nice word or both. Only this! Do not be ashamed!

***

Evening

• Repeat STOP to stop thinking.

- Say slowly to stop thinking: sun, flower, seven, path, tee, run, yellow, apple, fish, rain, pen, water, smile, talk, life, sky.
- Small supper.
- Nice talk (no complaints) 30 min. When nobody to talk with, phone or internet conversation oral or written.
- Walk 20 min.
- Imagine all the time people cannot wait to love you, but you must make the first step- a smile, a nice word or both. Only this! Do not be ashamed!

***

Night

Before sleep

- Take a shower (warm water) 1 min.
- Small physical excercise 5 min.

In Bed

- Repeat STOP (20 times)
- Say slowly untill you fall asleep: sun, flower, seven, path, tee, run, yellow, apple, fish, rain, pen, water, smile, talk, life, sky.

If you cannot fall asleep

- Say slowly untill you fall asleep: sun, flower, seven, path, tee, run, yellow, apple, fish, rain, pen, water, smile, talk, life, sky.

If above does not help

- Stand up and go to the toilet (when possible with as little light as possible)
- Say slowly untill you fall asleep: sun, flower, seven, path, tee, run, yellow, apple, fish, rain, pen, water, smile, talk, life, sky.

If above does not help

- Say STOP untill you fall asleep

If above does not help

- Go to the kitchen and have a very small snack.
- Back to the bed say slowly untill you fall asleep: sun, flower, seven, path, tee, run, yellow, apple, fish, rain, pen, water, smile, talk, life, sky.

If above does not help

- Say slowly untill morning: sun, flower, seven, path, tee, run, yellow, apple, fish, rain, pen, water, smile, talk, life, sky.

***

Day 3

Morning

* Repeat STOP (10 times every hour)

* Say slowly every 2 hours: sun, flower, seven, path, tee, run, yellow, apple, fish, rain, pen, water, smile, talk, life, sky.

* Small physical excercise (20 min)

* Small breakfast.

* Nice talk (no complaints) 30 min. When nobody to talk with, phone or internet conversation oral or written.

* Walk 30 min.

* Imagine all the time people cannot wait to love you, but you must make the first step- a smile, a nice word or both. Only this! Do not be ashamed!

***

Afternoon

* Repeat STOP (10 times every hour)

* Say slowly every 2 hours: sun, flower, seven, path, tee, run, yellow, apple, fish, rain, pen, water, smile, talk, life, sky.

* Dinner and half an hour break (you can sleep).

* Nice talk (no complaints) 30 min. When nobody to talk with, phone or internet conversation oral or written.

* Walk 30 min.

* Imagine all the time people cannot wait to love you, but you must make the first step- a smile, a nice word or both. Only this! Do not be ashamed!

***

Evening

- Repeat STOP to stop thinking.
- Say slowly to stop thinking: sun, flower, seven, path, tee, run, yellow, apple, fish, rain, pen, water, smile, talk, life, sky.
- Small supper.
- Nice talk (no complaints) 30 min. When nobody to talk with, phone or internet conversation oral or written.
- Walk 20 min.
- Imagine all the time people cannot wait to love you, but you must make the first step- a smile, a nice word or both. Only this! Do not be ashamed!

***

Night

Before sleep

- Take a shower (warm water) 1 min.
- Small physical excercise 5 min.

In Bed

- Repeat STOP (20 times)
- Say slowly untill you fall asleep: sun, flower, seven, path, tee, run, yellow, apple, fish, rain, pen, water, smile, talk, life, sky.

If you cannot fall asleep

- Say slowly untill you fall asleep: sun, flower, seven, path, tee, run, yellow, apple, fish, rain, pen, water, smile, talk, life, sky.

If above does not help

- Stand up and go to the toilet (when possible with as little light as possible)
- Say slowly untill you fall asleep: sun, flower, seven, path, tee, run, yellow, apple, fish, rain, pen, water, smile, talk, life, sky.

If above does not help

- Say STOP untill you fall asleep

If above does not help

- Go to the kitchen and have a very small snack.
- Back to the bed say slowly untill you fall asleep: sun, flower, seven, path, tee, run, yellow, apple, fish, rain, pen, water, smile, talk, life, sky.

If above does not help

- Say slowly untill morning: sun, flower, seven, path, tee, run, yellow, apple, fish, rain, pen, water, smile, talk, life, sky.

***

Day 4

Morning

* Repeat STOP (10 times every hour)

* Say slowly every 2 hours: sun, flower, seven, path, tee, run, yellow, apple, fish, rain, pen, water, smile, talk, life, sky.

* Small physical excercise (20 min)

* Small breakfast.

* Nice talk (no complaints) 30 min. When nobody to talk with, phone or internet conversation oral or written.

* Walk 30 min.

* Imagine all the time people cannot wait to love you, but you must make the first step- a smile, a nice word or both. Only this! Do not be ashamed!

***

Afternoon

* Repeat STOP (10 times every hour)

* Say slowly every 2 hours: sun, flower, seven, path, tee, run, yellow, apple, fish, rain, pen, water, smile, talk, life, sky.

* Dinner and half an hour break (you can sleep).

* Nice talk (no complaints) 30 min. When nobody to talk with, phone or internet conversation oral or written.

* Walk 30 min.

* Imagine all the time people cannot wait to love you, but you must make the first step- a smile, a nice word or both. Only this! Do not be ashamed!

***

Evening

* Repeat STOP to stop thinking.

- Say slowly to stop thinking: sun, flower, seven, path, tee, run, yellow, apple, fish, rain, pen, water, smile, talk, life, sky.
- Small supper.
- Nice talk (no complaints) 30 min. When nobody to talk with, phone or internet conversation oral or written.
- Walk 20 min.
- Imagine all the time people cannot wait to love you, but you must make the first step- a smile, a nice word or both. Only this! Do not be ashamed!

***

Night

Before sleep

- Take a shower (warm water) 1 min.
- Small physical excercise 5 min.

In Bed

- Repeat STOP (20 times)
- Say slowly untill you fall asleep: sun, flower, seven, path, tee, run, yellow, apple, fish, rain, pen, water, smile, talk, life, sky.

If you cannot fall asleep

- Say slowly untill you fall asleep: sun, flower, seven, path, tee, run, yellow, apple, fish, rain, pen, water, smile, talk, life, sky.

If above does not help

- Stand up and go to the toilet (when possible with as little light as possible)
- Say slowly untill you fall asleep: sun, flower, seven, path, tee, run, yellow, apple, fish, rain, pen, water, smile, talk, life, sky.

If above does not help

- Say STOP untill you fall asleep

If above does not help

- Go to the kitchen and have a very small snack.
- Back to the bed say slowly untill you fall asleep: sun, flower, seven, path, tee, run, yellow, apple, fish, rain, pen, water, smile, talk, life, sky.

If above does not help

- Say slowly untill morning: sun, flower, seven, path, tee, run, yellow, apple, fish, rain, pen, water, smile, talk, life, sky.

***

Day 5

Morning

* Repeat STOP (10 times every hour)

* Say slowly every 2 hours: sun, flower, seven, path, tee, run, yellow, apple, fish, rain, pen, water, smile, talk, life, sky.

* Small physical excercise (20 min)

* Small breakfast.

* Nice talk (no complaints) 30 min. When nobody to talk with, phone or internet conversation oral or written.

* Walk 30 min.

* Imagine all the time people cannot wait to love you, but you must make the first step- a smile, a nice word or both. Only this! Do not be ashamed!

***

Afternoon

* Repeat STOP (10 times every hour)

* Say slowly every 2 hours: sun, flower, seven, path, tee, run, yellow, apple, fish, rain, pen, water, smile, talk, life, sky.

* Dinner and half an hour break (you can sleep).

* Nice talk (no complaints) 30 min. When nobody to talk with, phone or internet conversation oral or written.

* Walk 30 min.

* Imagine all the time people cannot wait to love you, but you must make the first step- a smile, a nice word or both. Only this! Do not be ashamed!

***

Evening

- Repeat STOP to stop thinking.
- Say slowly to stop thinking: sun, flower, seven, path, tee, run, yellow, apple, fish, rain, pen, water, smile, talk, life, sky.
- Small supper.
- Nice talk (no complaints) 30 min. When nobody to talk with, phone or internet conversation oral or written.
- Walk 20 min.
- Imagine all the time people cannot wait to love you, but you must make the first step- a smile, a nice word or both. Only this! Do not be ashamed!

***

Night

Before sleep

- Take a shower (warm water) 1 min.
- Small physical excercise 5 min.

In Bed

- Repeat STOP (20 times)
- Say slowly untill you fall asleep: sun, flower, seven, path, tee, run, yellow, apple, fish, rain, pen, water, smile, talk, life, sky.

If you cannot fall asleep

- Say slowly untill you fall asleep: sun, flower, seven, path, tee, run, yellow, apple, fish, rain, pen, water, smile, talk, life, sky.

If above does not help

- Stand up and go to the toilet (when possible with as little light as possible)
- Say slowly untill you fall asleep: sun, flower, seven, path, tee, run, yellow, apple, fish, rain, pen, water, smile, talk, life, sky.

If above does not help

- Say STOP untill you fall asleep

If above does not help

- Go to the kitchen and have a very small snack.
- Back to the bed say slowly untill you fall asleep: sun, flower, seven, path, tee, run, yellow, apple, fish, rain, pen, water, smile, talk, life, sky.

If above does not help

- Say slowly untill morning: sun, flower, seven, path, tee, run, yellow, apple, fish, rain, pen, water, smile, talk, life, sky.

***

Day 6

Morning

* Repeat STOP (10 times every hour)

* Say slowly every 2 hours: sun, flower, seven, path, tee, run, yellow, apple, fish, rain, pen, water, smile, talk, life, sky.

* Small physical excercise (20 min)

* Small breakfast.

* Nice talk (no complaints) 30 min. When nobody to talk with, phone or internet conversation oral or written.

* Walk 30 min.

* Imagine all the time people cannot wait to love you, but you must make the first step- a smile, a nice word or both. Only this! Do not be ashamed!

***

Afternoon

* Repeat STOP (10 times every hour)

* Say slowly every 2 hours: sun, flower, seven, path, tee, run, yellow, apple, fish, rain, pen, water, smile, talk, life, sky.

* Dinner and half an hour break (you can sleep).

* Nice talk (no complaints) 30 min. When nobody to talk with, phone or internet conversation oral or written.

* Walk 30 min.

* Imagine all the time people cannot wait to love you, but you must make the first step- a smile, a nice word or both. Only this! Do not be ashamed!

***

Evening

- Repeat STOP to stop thinking.

- Say slowly to stop thinking: sun, flower, seven, path, tee, run, yellow, apple, fish, rain, pen, water, smile, talk, life, sky.
- Small supper.
- Nice talk (no complaints) 30 min. When nobody to talk with, phone or internet conversation oral or written.
- Walk 20 min.
- Imagine all the time people cannot wait to love you, but you must make the first step- a smile, a nice word or both. Only this! Do not be ashamed!

***

Night

Before sleep

- Take a shower (warm water) 1 min.
- Small physical excercise 5 min.

In Bed

- Repeat STOP (20 times)
- Say slowly untill you fall asleep: sun, flower, seven, path, tee, run, yellow, apple, fish, rain, pen, water, smile, talk, life, sky.

If you cannot fall asleep

- Say slowly untill you fall asleep: sun, flower, seven, path, tee, run, yellow, apple, fish, rain, pen, water, smile, talk, life, sky.

If above does not help

- Stand up and go to the toilet (when possible with as little light as possible)
- Say slowly untill you fall asleep: sun, flower, seven, path, tee, run, yellow, apple, fish, rain, pen, water, smile, talk, life, sky.

If above does not help

- Say STOP untill you fall asleep

If above does not help

- Go to the kitchen and have a very small snack.
- Back to the bed say slowly untill you fall asleep: sun, flower, seven, path, tee, run, yellow, apple, fish, rain, pen, water, smile, talk, life, sky.

If above does not help

- Say slowly untill morning: sun, flower, seven, path, tee, run, yellow, apple, fish, rain, pen, water, smile, talk, life, sky.

***

Day 7

Morning

* Repeat STOP (10 times every hour)

* Say slowly every 2 hours: sun, flower, seven, path, tee, run, yellow, apple, fish, rain, pen, water, smile, talk, life, sky.

* Small physical excercise (20 min)

* Small breakfast.

* Nice talk (no complaints) 30 min. When nobody to talk with, phone or internet conversation oral or written.

* Walk 30 min.

* Imagine all the time people cannot wait to love you, but you must make the first step- a smile, a nice word or both. Only this! Do not be ashamed!

***

Afternoon

* Repeat STOP (10 times every hour)

* Say slowly every 2 hours: sun, flower, seven, path, tee, run, yellow, apple, fish, rain, pen, water, smile, talk, life, sky.

* Dinner and half an hour break (you can sleep).

* Nice talk (no complaints) 30 min. When nobody to talk with, phone or internet conversation oral or written.

* Walk 30 min.

* Imagine all the time people cannot wait to love you, but you must make the first step- a smile, a nice word or both. Only this! Do not be ashamed!

***

Evening

- Repeat STOP to stop thinking.
- Say slowly to stop thinking: sun, flower, seven, path, tee, run, yellow, apple, fish, rain, pen, water, smile, talk, life, sky.
- Small supper.
- Nice talk (no complaints) 30 min. When nobody to talk with, phone or internet conversation oral or written.
- Walk 20 min.
- Imagine all the time people cannot wait to love you, but you must make the first step- a smile, a nice word or both. Only this! Do not be ashamed!

***

Night

Before sleep

- Take a shower (warm water) 1 min.
- Small physical excercise 5 min.

In Bed

- Repeat STOP (20 times)
- Say slowly untill you fall asleep: sun, flower, seven, path, tee, run, yellow, apple, fish, rain, pen, water, smile, talk, life, sky.

If you cannot fall asleep

- Say slowly untill you fall asleep: sun, flower, seven, path, tee, run, yellow, apple, fish, rain, pen, water, smile, talk, life, sky.

If above does not help

- Stand up and go to the toilet (when possible with as little light as possible)
- Say slowly untill you fall asleep: sun, flower, seven, path, tee, run, yellow, apple, fish, rain, pen, water, smile, talk, life, sky.

If above does not help

- Say STOP untill you fall asleep

If above does not help

- Go to the kitchen and have a very small snack.
- Back to the bed say slowly untill you fall asleep: sun, flower, seven, path, tee, run, yellow, apple, fish, rain, pen, water, smile, talk, life, sky.

If above does not help

- Say slowly untill morning: sun, flower, seven, path, tee, run, yellow, apple, fish, rain, pen, water, smile, talk, life, sky.

***

Congratulations! You made the therapy and should be happy now. Remember, repeat this Self Anxiety Therapy SAT every time in the future you become anxious again during longer than 2 weeks.

P. W. Ariveder

9 798674 247562